Tigers in Trouble

Louise Spilsbury

Contents

Collins

Tigers

Tigers are the largest of all the big cats.
There were once 100,000 tigers in the world.

Now there are just 3,000 tigers.
Why are tigers in trouble?

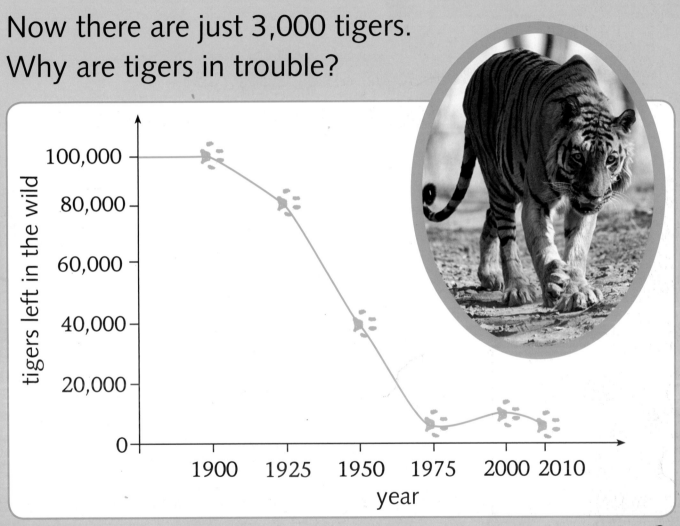

Tiger habitats

Many tigers live in habitats with trees and long grass.
They can hide in the grass.

People cut down trees and grass
to build new houses and farms.
Without their habitat, tigers have
nowhere to hide.

5

Tiger prey

Tigers need grass to hide in when they hunt deer and other prey.

6

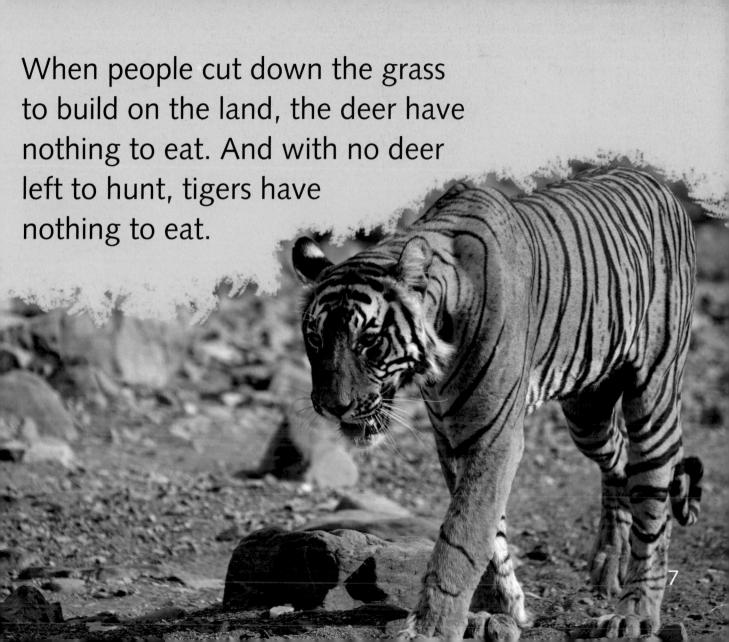

When people cut down the grass
to build on the land, the deer have
nothing to eat. And with no deer
left to hunt, tigers have
nothing to eat.

Tigers in danger

Poachers are people who put traps out to catch tigers.

trap

Poachers sell tiger skins for lots of money. Some people put tiger skins in their homes.

Some poachers sell tiger bones.

bones used for medicine

People make medicines from tiger bones.

medicine packets

Help for tigers

To help tigers, people set up reserves.

Tigers live, hide and hunt deer safely in reserves.

13

How many tigers are in the wild?

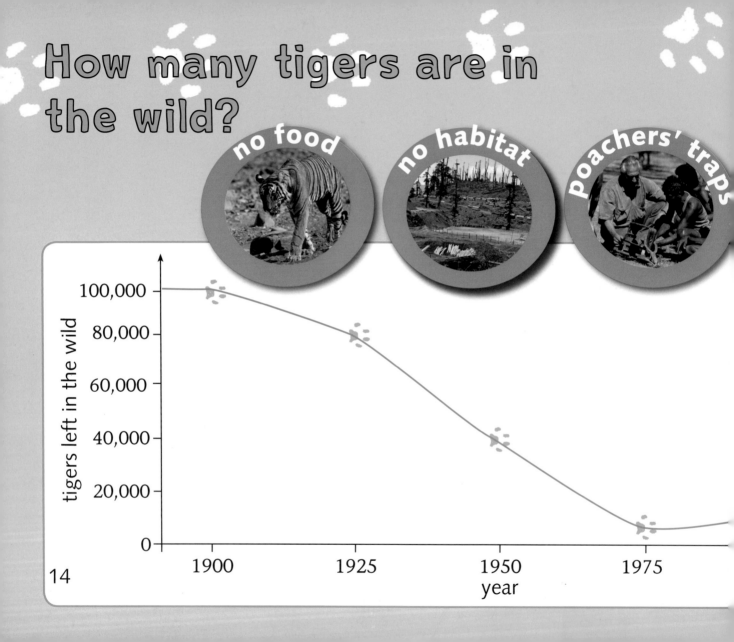

no food

no habitat

poachers' traps

tigers left in the wild

100,000

80,000

60,000

40,000

20,000

0

1900   1925   1950   1975

year

Index

reserves

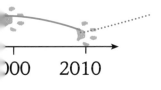

000   2010

Ideas for reading

Written by Gillian Howell
Primary Literacy Consultant

Learning objectives: *(reading objectives correspond with Blue band; all other objectives correspond with Copper band)* use phonics to read unknown or difficult words; identify and make notes of the main points of sections of text; identify how different texts are organised; identify features that writers use to provoke readers' reactions; sustain conversation, explaining or giving reasons for their views or choices; use layout, format, graphics, illustrations for different purposes

Curriculum links: Citizenship: Animals and us

High frequency words: are, the, of, all, big, cats, there, were, once, in, now, just, many, live, with, trees, and, they, can, people, down, to, new, houses, and, their, have, when, on, no, who, put, out, for, some, homes, make, from, help, up

Interest words: habitats, prey, danger, poachers, medicines, reserves

Resources: paper, pens, pencils, paint

Word count: 177

Getting started

- Read the title together and look at the front cover. Ask the children what first impression the cover photograph gives them. Talk about the title. What sort of trouble do they think tigers are in, and why?

- Turn to the back cover and read the blurb together. Were the children's ideas about tigers correct?

- Ask the children to read the contents page aloud. If children struggle with any of the words, for example, *habitat,* remind them to chop the words into sounds and then blend them together again.

- Ask the children if they think it will make any difference to the information if they read chapters in sequence or dip in to particular chapters that interest them first. Flick quickly through the book to elicit that the information develops throughout the book, so it should be read in sequence.

Reading and responding

- Ask the children to read the text aloud but in a quiet voice and make notes of key points that affect tiger populations. Listen in to the children and prompt as necessary.